A NOTE TO PARENTS

When your children are ready to "step into reading," giving them the right books—and lots of them—is as crucial as giving them the right food to eat. **Step into Reading Books** present exciting stories and information reinforced with lively, colorful illustrations that make learning to read fun, satisfying, and worthwhile. They are priced so that acquiring an entire library of them is affordable. And they are beginning readers with an important difference—they're written on four levels.

Step 1 Books, with their very large type and extremely simple vocabulary, have been created for the very youngest readers. **Step 2 Books** are both longer and slightly more difficult. **Step 3 Books,** written to mid-second-grade reading levels, are for the child who has acquired even greater reading skills. **Step 4 Books** offer exciting nonfiction for the increasingly proficient reader.

Children develop at different ages. **Step into Reading Books,** with their four levels of reading, are designed to help children become good—and interested—readers *faster.* The grade levels assigned to the four steps—preschool through grade 1 for Step 1, grades 1 through 3 for Step 2, grades 2 and 3 for Step 3, and grades 2 through 4 for Step 4—are intended only as guides. Some children move through all four steps very rapidly; others climb the steps over a period of several years. These books will help your child "step into reading" in style!

For Chloe
—A.G.

For my family
—C.S.

Photo credits: pp. 6, 7, 16, 25, 36–37, National Baseball Library, Cooperstown, N.Y.; p. 27, AP/Wide World Photos; pp. 33, 41, 45, UPI/Bettmann Newsphotos.

Text copyright © 1990 by Andrew Gutelle. Illustrations copyright © 1990 by Cliff Spohn. All rights reserved under International and Pan-American Copyright Conventions. Published in the United States by Random House, Inc., New York, and simultaneously in Canada by Random House of Canada Limited, Toronto.

Library of Congress Cataloging-in-Publication Data
Gutelle, Andrew. Baseball's Best: Five True Stories by Andrew Gutelle. p. cm. –(Step into reading. A Step 4 book) Summary: Examines the accomplishments of Babe Ruth, Joe DiMaggio, Jackie Robinson, Roberto Clemente, and Hank Aaron, all of whom were elected to the Baseball Hall of Fame. ISBN 0-394-80983-1 (pbk.); 0-394-90983-6 (lib. bdg.) 1. Baseball players–United States–Biography–Juvenile literature. 2. National Baseball Hall of Fame and Museum–Juvenile literature. [1. Baseball players.] I. Title. II. Series. GV865.A1G84 1990
796.357'902'2–dc20 [B] 89-35413 [920] CIP AC

Manufactured in the United States of America   24 25 26 27 28 29 30

STEP INTO READING is a trademark of Random House, Inc.

Step into Reading

BASEBALL'S BEST

Five True Stories

By Andrew Gutelle
Illustrated by Cliff Spohn

A Step 4 Book

Random House 🏠 New York

The Hall of Fame

Every year hundreds of thousands of people visit Cooperstown, New York. What makes this quiet little town so special? It is the home of the Baseball Hall of Fame, a museum that honors more than two hundred of the greatest stars who ever played the game.

Each of these home-run hitters, record breakers, and World Series winners has a story that got him where he is—in the Hall of Fame. Here are five of those stories—thrilling, incredible, and absolutely true.

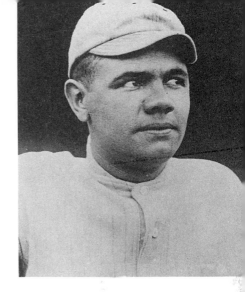

1

The Babe Calls His Shot

It's the third game of the 1932 World Series. The mighty New York Yankees have come to Chicago to play the Cubs. The Yankees have already won the first two games of the Series. The Cubs must win today if they are to have any chance at all of becoming world champs.

Fifty thousand loyal Cub fans pack Wrigley Field. They know that the Yankees and their fans heckled and embarrassed the Cubs in New York. Now it's their turn. The Chicago rooters have prepared a nasty welcome for the Yankees and especially for the greatest Yankee of them all—Babe Ruth.

George Herman Ruth has been playing major-league ball since 1914. As a pitcher, Babe helps hurl the Boston Red Sox to two world championships. But what really catches everyone's attention is his hitting. Babe can sock a baseball out of sight!

When Ruth is traded to the Yankees, he moves from the pitcher's mound to the outfield and takes New York City by storm. So many fans want to see him play that after a few years the team builds a new, bigger ballpark. In the very first game there the Babe drills a game-winning homer into the upper deck. No wonder everyone soon starts calling Yankee Stadium "The House That Ruth Built."

Ruth is baseball's first superstar. His cocky and confident style has made him the most colorful player ever to step into the batter's box. But some claim that he is getting old and is no longer the player he once was. Fans wonder whether he will be able to make the difference in this crucial game.

Now, as the Yankees take the field in their showdown with the Cubs, the crowd boos Ruth. But the Babe just laughs. He and teammate Lou Gehrig take batting practice. As the Cub fans watch, the two sluggers knock one ball after another into the bleachers. This show of Yankee power makes the fans madder. When the Babe trots out to left field to warm up, the fans hurl lemons at him. "Get off the field, old-timer!" they shout.

The game begins. In the very first inning Ruth shows what he's got left. He smacks a home run to put the Yankees ahead 3–0. But the Cubs fight back. In the fourth inning a Cub batter hits a sinking line drive to left field.

Babe races in and tries to catch the ball before it bounces. To the delight of the crowd, the ball rolls past him for a double. That helps the Cubs tie the score. Suddenly the outcome of the game—and the Series—is in doubt.

In the fifth inning Ruth is again at bat. The crowd is roaring at him. The Cub players are shouting from the bench, too. Ruth looks up at the stands, calm and cool as ever. The first pitch from Charlie Root is a strike. But Ruth does not swing. Instead, he holds up a finger as if to say, "That's one." Soon Root zips another strike past Ruth. Now Babe holds up two fingers. One more strike to go.

The crowd is really going wild. Ruth shouts something at the Cubs' bench. He seems to be pointing to a flagpole in the center-field bleachers. It's as if he's saying to the pitcher, "I'm going to drill the next ball you throw into the bleachers, and you can't stop me!"

Ruth steps back into the batter's box. Root goes into his wind-up. He pitches. Ruth swings and there is a loud crack! The ball blasts off Ruth's bat. Like a rocket it soars to

center field. The ball sails into the bleachers and lands a few feet from the flagpole. It has gone just where the Babe said it would!

Ruth circles the bases. For a moment the stunned crowd is silent. Then Yankee fans *and* Cub fans rise to their feet and applaud. They can't help themselves. Ruth has performed an incredible feat. Does any other player have such nerve or talent? He has challenged the Cubs and their fans and won. The Yankees go on to take the game. The next day they win again to sweep the Series.

"Suppose you hadn't connected?" a reporter asks Ruth after the game.

"I never thought of that," says Babe. "I surely would have looked like a fool."

So many years have passed since the Bambino hit that one-in-a-million homer. Now it has become part of legend—one of the best sports stories ever. But many fans and baseball historians still wonder. Did Babe Ruth really call his shot?

In the noise and excitement it was hard to know for certain. In 1932 there was no television. No one can look at the instant replay to decide. The only "proof" is a home movie taken by a fan in the stands that day. It shows for certain that the Babe was up to something in the batter's box. But exactly what was he doing? That remains a mystery.

Even the players on the field disagree about what happened that day. Cubs pitcher Charlie Root says, "If he had tried to show me up like that, I'd knock him on the seat of his pants!" But many of Ruth's teammates insist that he called his shot.

Of course only one man knew for sure what happened that day. That was Babe Ruth himself. But the Babe never did set the record straight. He loved to tell people how he called his shot—but the story did change a little every time he told it. Sometimes he hinted that he didn't call it. "All I wanted to do was give the ball a ride out of the ballpark anywhere," he told one reporter.

Well, maybe Babe Ruth called his shot and maybe he didn't. Either way, one thing is certain. The Babe stepped onto the field that day in Chicago with two things in mind. He wanted to have a little fun, and he wanted to give the fans their money's worth. And that's just what he did!

2

Joltin' Joe's Amazing Streak

On May 15, 1941, the seats at Yankee Stadium are filled with nervous fans. The season is a month old, and the "Bronx Bombers" are struggling. The team is stuck in fourth place. To make matters worse, Joe DiMaggio, the star Yankee outfielder, is in a hitting slump.

Joe has been with the Yankees since 1936, when he was twenty-two years old. After five years he is one of baseball's best all-around players. The sizzling line drives DiMaggio hits earn him the nickname Joltin' Joe.

As the fans settle into their seats they

wonder: Will today be the day Joe snaps out of his slump?

In the first inning they get their answer. Joe steps up and rips a single to left field.

The Yankees end up beating the Chicago White Sox. The hometown crowd is happy. But there is something they do not know. They have witnessed the start of the most amazing batting streak in baseball history.

The next day Joe smacks a triple and a home run. With each passing game Joe gets at least one hit. After three weeks, he has hit in twenty straight games. Fans everywhere begin to notice. Each day they check their newspapers to see if Joe has gotten a hit. Is he going to set a new major-league record?

To do that Joe will have to go one better than George Sisler, who hit in forty-one straight games in 1922. Sisler has held the modern record for almost twenty years. But when DiMaggio's streak soars past thirty-five games, fans realize that he may shatter Sisler's mark. Sisler himself says, "If anyone ever breaks my record, I hope it's Joe."

On June 29 the Yankees are set to play a doubleheader against the Washington Senators. Joe needs a hit in each game to break the record. Over 31,000 fans have come to see if Joe can make it. They sit in blistering heat. But even when the temperature climbs to almost a hundred degrees, Joe keeps his cool. In his third at bat of the first game he doubles. That hit ties the record.

Between games Joe tries to take it easy in the clubhouse. Then the second game starts. One more hit and DiMaggio will break the record. The pressure on Joe is tremendous.

As Joe returns to the dugout, he makes a terrible discovery. His favorite bat is missing! It has been stolen by a fan hunting for a souvenir. Whenever Joe has had one last chance to keep the streak going, that was the bat he used. "That bat was just right for me," says Joe. "I liked the feel of it."

Joe tries one of his other bats and pops out in the first inning. When he gets up in the third, he hits a weak grounder for another out.

Is Joe still thinking about his missing bat? Yankee right fielder Tommy Henrich offers Joe his bat. "Maybe my bat will change your luck," he says. But Joe decides to stick with the one he has been using and pops up again.

Now it's the seventh inning. This may be Joe's last chance to keep the streak alive. He decides to give Henrich's bat a try.

Joe steps up to the plate. Pitcher Red Anderson starts Joe off with an inside fastball. "Ball one!" shouts the ump. Now Anderson tries a curveball. As it crosses the plate, the ball is spinning away from Joe. With a snap of his wrists, Joe flashes the bat across the plate. He rips the ball into left field. It's a clean single! The crowd leaps to its feet and cheers. In the dugout his teammates wave and shout at baseball's newest record holder.

Joe has done it! But the amazing thing is he keeps on doing it. With the pressure off, the streak rolls on. By July 17, Joe has hit in fifty-six games in a row. That night over 67,000 fans jam into Cleveland's Municipal Stadium.

In his first at bat Joe smashes a ball over the third-base bag. Ken Keltner darts to his

right. With a backhand stab he grabs the ball.
His throw to first base nips Joe by a step.

Joe hits the ball hard all night, but always
right at a fielder. When he steps up to home
plate in the eighth inning, everyone knows
this is his last chance to keep the streak alive.

Joe works the count to one ball and one
strike. When pitcher Jim Bagby fires a
fastball, Joe swings and sends a hard ground

ball up the middle. Shortstop Lou Boudreau fields it and flips to second. The second baseman throws on to first for a double play. The inning is over, and so is the streak.

Joe slowly trots back to the dugout and picks up his glove. He goes back onto the field, and the fans begin to cheer. By the time Joe reaches center field, every fan is standing and cheering. The crowd keeps on cheering Joe for several minutes. The fans in Cleveland want DiMaggio to know that everyone has been thrilled by what he has done.

After the game Joe talks about the streak. "I can't say I'm glad it's over," he says. "Of course I wanted it to go on as long as it could. Now that it's over, I just want to get out there and keep winning ball games."

The Yankees go on to win the pennant and the World Series. For his incredible performance during the season, Joe is named the Most Valuable Player.

Joe DiMaggio's streak won him the respect of baseball fans everywhere. Since then some players have hit in more than thirty straight games. Pete Rose even pushed his streak past forty games. But no one has come close to Joe's magic number of fifty-six.

3

The First

It is opening day in 1947. At Ebbets Field, the home of the Brooklyn Dodgers, a rookie is making history. His name is Jackie Robinson, and he is the first black man on a major-league team in more than half a century.

When pro baseball began, a few black men played with white players. But over the years, that stopped. By 1900, team owners decide that major-league baseball will be for whites only. Black ballplayers are forced to start their own teams and play in separate leagues.

Black teams have always had some great players in their line-ups. And Branch Rickey, who has been in charge of the Brooklyn Dodgers since 1942, knows this. He would like to have some of these players on his team.

Rickey figures it's time for blacks and whites to play baseball together again. So he sends his scouts to the black teams to look for the right man.

It will take a very special player to break baseball's "color barrier." Rickey wants someone with pride. But Rickey also needs someone who can take insults and not fight back. He must stand up for himself by showing how well he can do out on the field.

Jackie Robinson is a talented shortstop for an all-black team called the Kansas City Monarchs. A scout brings Robinson to meet Rickey. "I have reason to believe you're the man I have been looking for," says Rickey.

Jackie Robinson understands the challenge. "If you want to take this chance, I promise there will be no incident," he replies.

Robinson signs a Dodger contract. His first year is spent playing in the minor leagues for the Montreal Royals. He leads the Royals to the league championship. The next year, during spring training, Rickey announces that Robinson is ready for the majors.

"I'm thrilled," Jackie tells reporters. "This is the chance I've been waiting for."

On opening day 26,000 Dodger fans come to see Robinson. Many people wear "I'm for

Jackie" buttons. Jackie's wife, Rachel, and their son, Jack Jr., are in the stands too.

In the seventh inning the Dodgers trail by one run. With a man on base Jackie bunts. The fielder rushes to make a play on the speedy Robinson. The throw is wild, and Jackie is safe on an error. When the next batter doubles, Jackie scores. The first run of his Dodger career helps win the game.

As a hitter, Jackie gets off to a slow start. Like most rookies he has trouble batting against top major-league pitchers. To make matters worse, he must battle prejudice wherever he goes. Some opposing players shout curses at him from the bench, while others threaten to strike if Jackie takes the field. Throughout the season players test his courage. Pitchers hurl fastballs dangerously close to his head. Runners slide with the spikes of their shoes aimed at his legs.

There are problems off the field too. In

parts of the South it is the law that blacks and whites must be kept apart. In some cities Robinson is not allowed to stay in the same hotels or eat in the same restaurants as his white teammates. As he travels through these parts of the country, Jackie receives hate mail. Some letters even threaten his life.

At first Robinson's teammates don't know how they feel about playing with him. But as they see the trouble he must face, their feelings change. They make sure that players and fans understand that Jackie is not just a black man playing baseball. He is a Dodger. "Having Jackie on the team is strange, just like anything else that's new," says one of his teammates. "But if he can help us win, I'm all for him. That's the only test."

As the season wears on, Robinson's hitting improves. And he gets to show off his greatest skill. Fans quickly discover that Jackie is the most exciting runner in baseball. As a former track star, he possesses blazing speed. But that is only part of the story. "Being daring—that's half my game," he explains.

When he gets on base, Robinson gives opposing pitchers fits. He dances off the base, challenging them to try and throw him out. If a pitcher tries to pick him off, Jackie scampers back to the base. Then he takes an even bigger lead, and the challenge begins again. When a pitcher ignores him, he steals the base.

As the months pass, Jackie gains respect. In spite of the pressures he faces, he has a brilliant season. He leads the league in stolen bases and is second in runs scored. The

Dodgers win the pennant and Robinson is voted Rookie of the Year.

Robinson's career lasts ten years. During that time the Dodgers win six pennants and one World Series. In 1956 Robinson announces he is retiring. "I'm glad my last season with the Dodgers was a good one," says Jackie. "Maybe I have another good season or two in me, but at thirty-eight you never know. I'm glad I'm ending strong."

Jackie Robinson had to wait until he was twenty-eight years old to get a chance to play in the major leagues. As a result, his career statistics do not match those of most great ballplayers. Others scored more runs and won more pennants. But no one accomplished more than he did. In 1962 Jackie Robinson is honored for his achievements on and off the playing field. He becomes the first black elected to the Hall of Fame.

4

Clemente's Last Hit

There is just one week left in the 1972 baseball season. The Pittsburgh Pirates are certain to finish in first place and make the National League play-offs. Now all attention turns to the Pirates' star outfielder, Roberto Clemente. Only nine players have ended their careers with 3,000 or more base hits. Clemente wants to become the tenth.

Clemente is from Puerto Rico. To the people who live there and in the rest of Latin America, he is a hero.

For seventeen years now Roberto has returned to Puerto Rico after each season. He spends the winter playing baseball and meeting his many fans. Clemente dreams of building a "sports city" in his homeland, where boys and girls will get a chance to play the game he loves.

Clemente is a proud man. For many years he has felt he has not gotten the credit he deserves. When people talk about baseball's greatest players, they name popular stars

like Willie Mays, Hank Aaron, and Mickey Mantle. Often they forget about Roberto.

Clemente gets his chance to prove what a great player he is in the 1971 World Series. After the Pirates lose the first two games to the Baltimore Orioles, Clemente leads his team back. He gets hits in every game, including a home run in the final contest. The Pirates win the World Series with Clemente named Most Valuable Player.

Now, as the 1972 season starts, Clemente has another goal to reach. If he can collect 118 more hits, he will reach the magic number of 3,000. But he is thirty-eight years old and has had many injuries. He misses many games. But Clemente pulls through with a late-season hitting surge. With just a few games left, his total is 2,999 hits!

The Pirates are playing against the New York Mets in Pittsburgh. In the first game Clemente hits a ground ball past the pitcher.

The Mets' second baseman barely gets to the ball. He bobbles it and then throws to first. Clemente beats the throw by a step.

The crowd turns to the scoreboard. The word "hit" is flashed. But then the official scorer changes his mind. He switches to "error." Clemente is angry. He feels cheated out of the most important hit of his career.

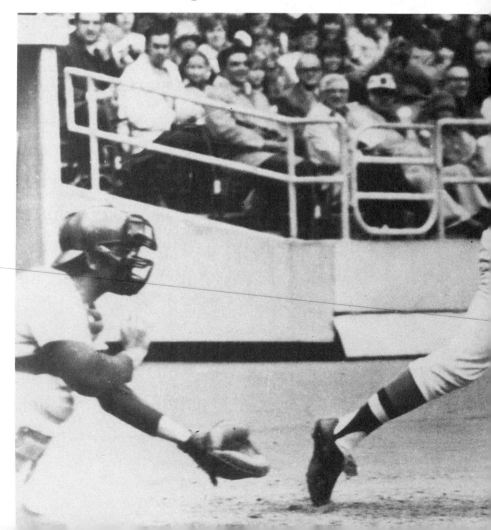

Clemente fails to get any hits. The next day he must try again. In the first inning he faces pitcher Jon Matlack. After throwing several fastballs, Matlack tosses a sharp-breaking curve. Clemente swings and strikes out.

The next time up, Matlack gets a strike on Clemente. Then he tries another curveball. This time Roberto is ready. He rips a line drive

into left field. It's base hit number 3,000!

The ball that he hit is taken out of play and presented to Clemente. It is a wonderful moment—a moment that he has worked long and hard for.

What he does not know is that this headline-making hit is to be the last regular-season hit of his career...and of his life.

After the season ends, Roberto once again returns to Puerto Rico. On Christmas Eve a terrible earthquake strikes the country of Nicaragua. Thousands of people are killed. Many others are homeless. The people of Puerto Rico want to help their neighbors, and Clemente agrees to be in charge.

A plane loaded with food and clothing will fly to Nicaragua on New Year's Eve. As the time approaches for the flight, Roberto hears some disturbing news. The supplies on other planes are being stolen when they arrive. Too little is reaching the hurt, homeless families who need it the most.

Clemente decides that only he can make sure that the supplies get to those who most need them. He cancels plans to spend the night with his family and friends. Instead he will fly to Nicaragua.

On New Year's Eve, Clemente's plane takes off. Moments later one of the engines explodes and catches fire. The plane plunges into the ocean. The people of Puerto Rico search the waters offshore, but it is no use. Roberto Clemente is never found.

The world is shocked by Clemente's death. Saddest of all are the children who looked up to him. In a New York City school third graders write essays about Roberto. Here is what one child says:

"The world should remember Roberto Clemente because he really cared. He cared enough to bring clothing and money to Nicaragua. He was truly a great man and will be remembered by millions. He will always be a hero."

Three months after his death, America's baseball writers gather. A player must be out of baseball for at least five years before he can be voted into the Hall of Fame. The writers decide that the rules can be broken. Roberto Clemente is elected to the Hall of Fame.

5

The New Home-Run King

It is April 1954. Playing right field for the Milwaukee Braves is a young rookie named Henry Aaron. Sometimes Aaron looks lost in the outfield. He makes few base hits. But manager Charlie Grimm is not worried. "Aaron is just trying too hard," he says. "He'll settle down. Someday he's going to be a great ballplayer." Grimm doesn't know how right he is!

On April 23, Aaron hits his first major-league homer. It is a special moment for a young player like Hank. But it can't compare with what will happen to him twenty years later.

In 1974 a new baseball season is beginning. No one seems to care about who will win the pennant. Fans want to know one thing: When will Hank Aaron of the Atlanta Braves pass Babe Ruth and become the new home-run king of baseball?

During his career Ruth smacked 714 round-trippers. People once thought that record would last forever. But going into the 1974 season "Hammerin' Hank" has hit 713!

No two people could be less alike than Babe Ruth and Hank Aaron. The Babe was a showman who loved being the center of attention. He didn't just hit home runs, he blasted them out of sight. Everything he did on or off the field made headlines.

Aaron, on the other hand, is a private person. He is a steady player, but he is rarely flashy. Hank is the most consistent home-run hitter who ever lived. He never comes close to hitting sixty homers in a season, as the Babe did. But year after year he knocks about forty baseballs over the fence.

For the past few seasons Aaron has been closing in on Ruth's record. As people realize Hank has a shot at the record, the pressure builds. Hank gets thousands of letters. IIis phone rings day and night.

The Braves open the season with three games in Cincinnati before returning home to Atlanta. The owner of the Braves does not want Hank to play in those first three games. It will be better for business and the loyal Braves fans if Hank breaks the record in front of the home crowd.

The commissioner of baseball disagrees. Records may be important, but there is a pennant race to think about. He says the Braves must play their best team in Cincinnati, and that includes Hank Aaron.

Some people wonder if Aaron will be trying hard in those first games. Hank answers the only way he knows how. On his first swing of the season he slams a home run. Now he has tied Babe Ruth's record.

"I have never gone on the field and given less than my level best," Aaron explains. Still, that is the only home run he hits in Cincinnati.

And so the Braves come home to Atlanta with the stage set for the history-making homer. On the night of April 8 there are 53,775 fans in the stands. Millions more are watching on television.

Aaron bats in the second inning. Los Angeles Dodger pitcher Al Downing is on the mound. Downing does not want to give up the most famous home run in baseball history. He pitches so carefully that Hank walks. The crowd boos.

Now it's the fourth inning. Aaron bats again. Downing's first pitch is a ball. Then he

tries to sneak a fastball past the man they call The Hammer. Aaron swings and hits a drive to left-center field.

Downing turns and sees his outfielders racing to the fence. "At first I didn't think it was going out," he later says. "But that ball kept carrying and carrying."

The ball is heading for the Atlanta Braves' bullpen, where some of the players are watching Hank bat. The crowd leaps to its feet as the ball sails over the fence for a home run!

In the television booth, sportscaster Milo Hamilton is describing the action. "It's gone!" he shouts into his microphone. "It's seven–fifteen! Baseball has a new home-run champion. It's Henry Aaron!"

The fans are going wild. Braves players are pouring onto the field. There's only one person in the entire ballpark who seems calm—Henry Aaron. As he has 714 times before, Hank trots around the bases. Finally, when Hank rounds third, his emotions show through. He sees his teammates, his wife, and his parents all waiting at home plate to greet him, and he breaks out in a huge smile. When he touches the plate, the players lift him on their shoulders.

After the game, three hundred reporters are waiting for Aaron. They have come from as far away as Japan. "I just thank God it's over," he tells them. "I feel I can relax now. I just want to have a great season."

Hank hits eighteen more homers that year. In the next two seasons he pushes his total to 755 before retiring and joining Babe Ruth in the Baseball Hall of Fame.